The Picture Book of
Deers

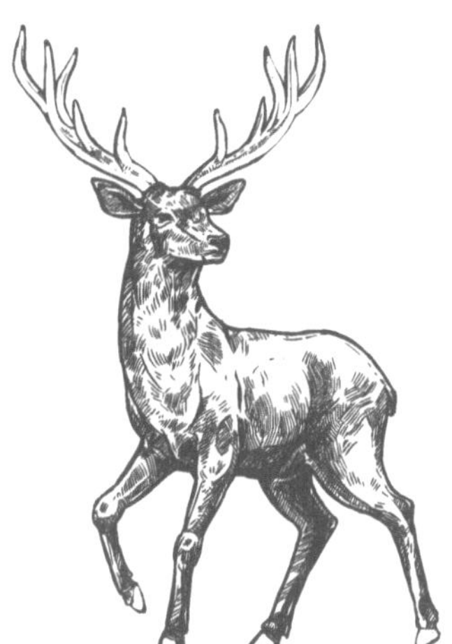

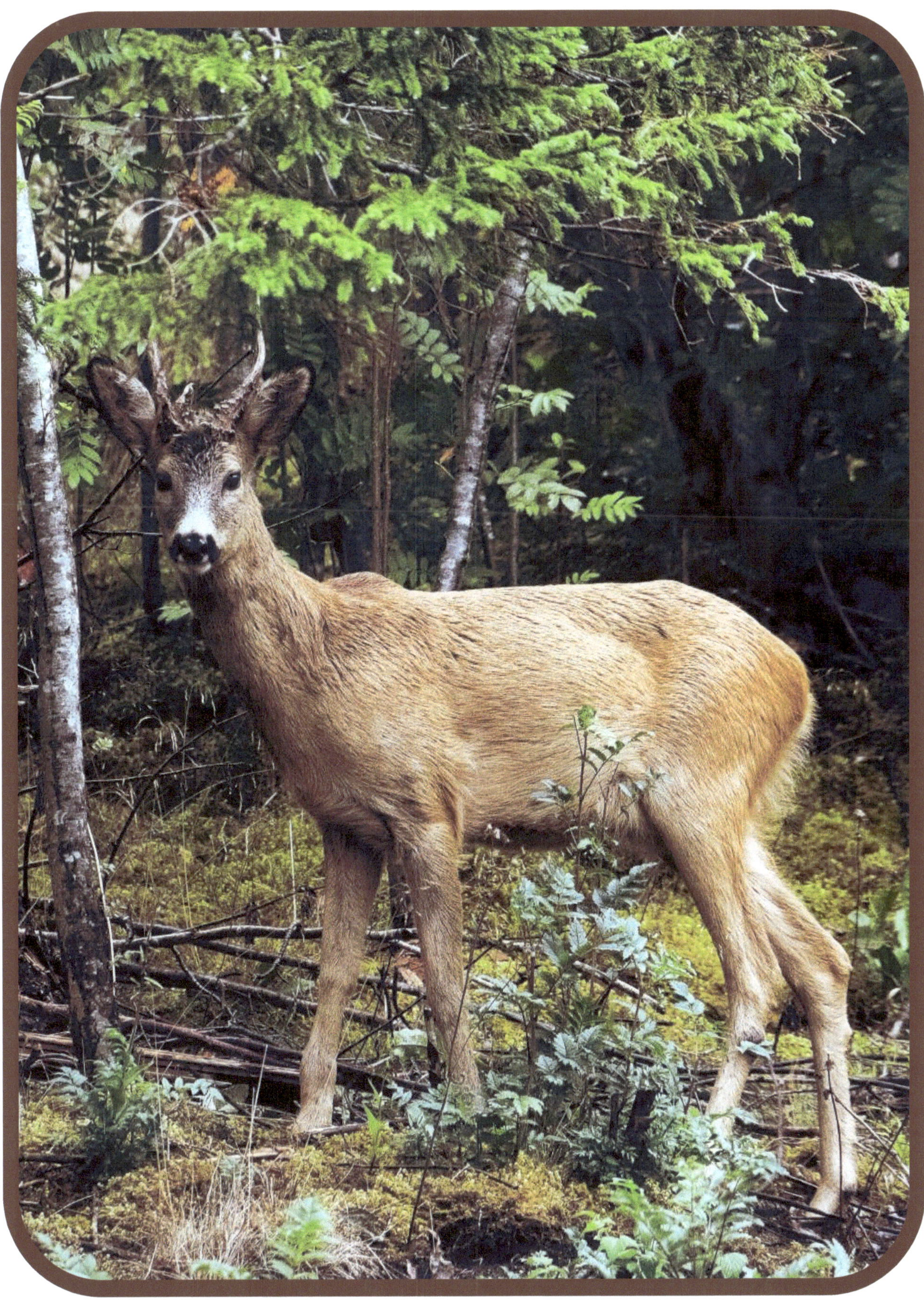

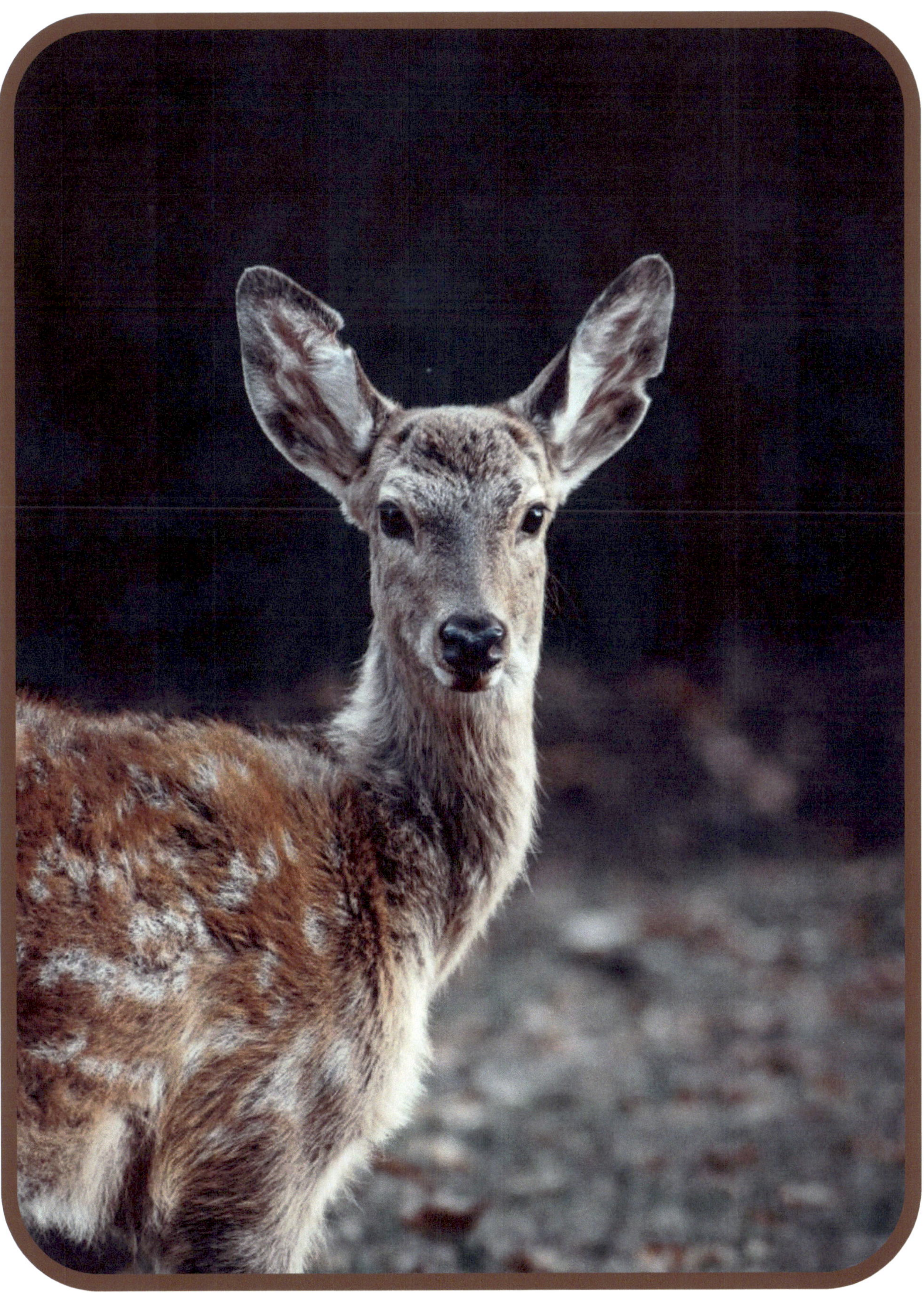

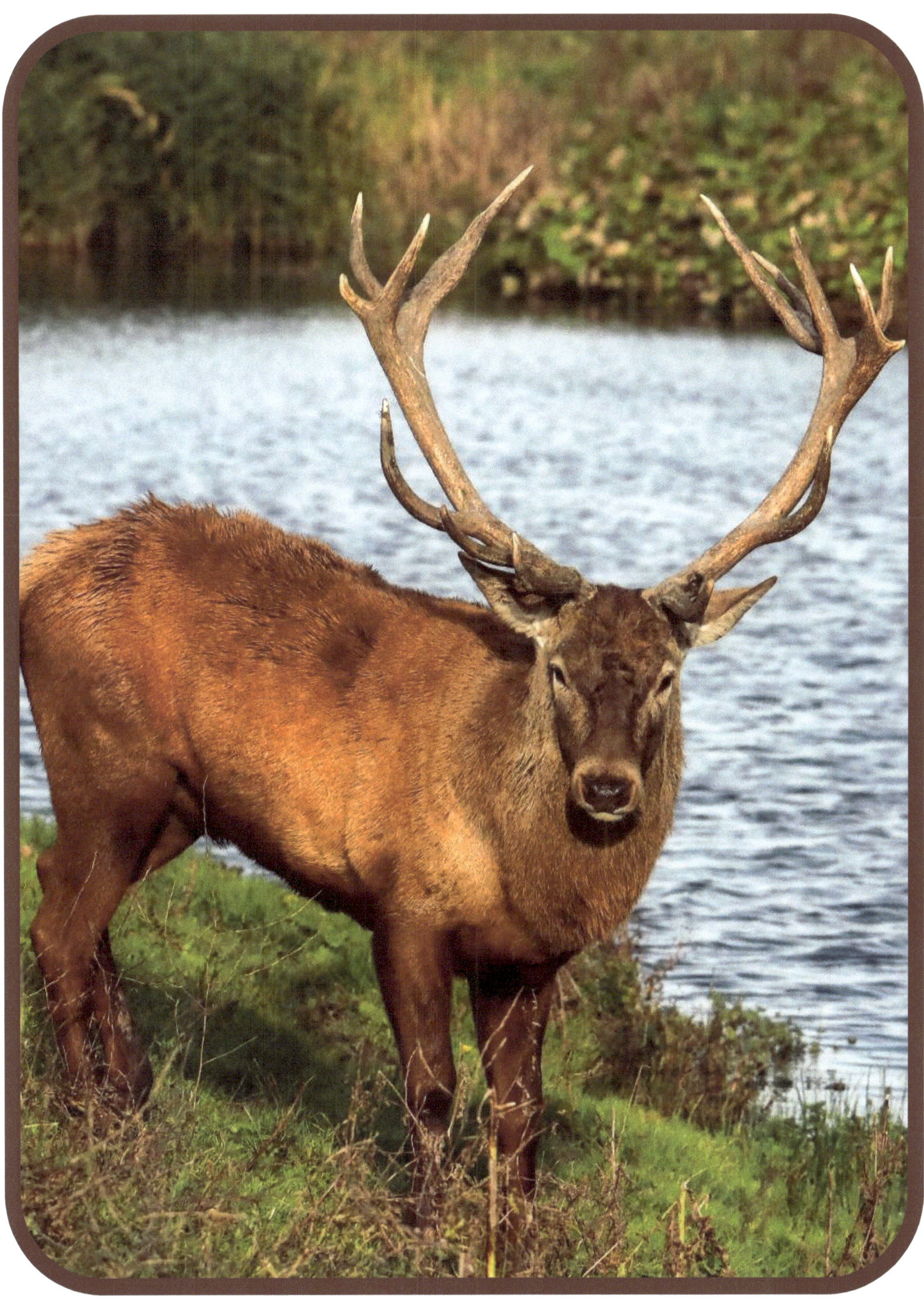

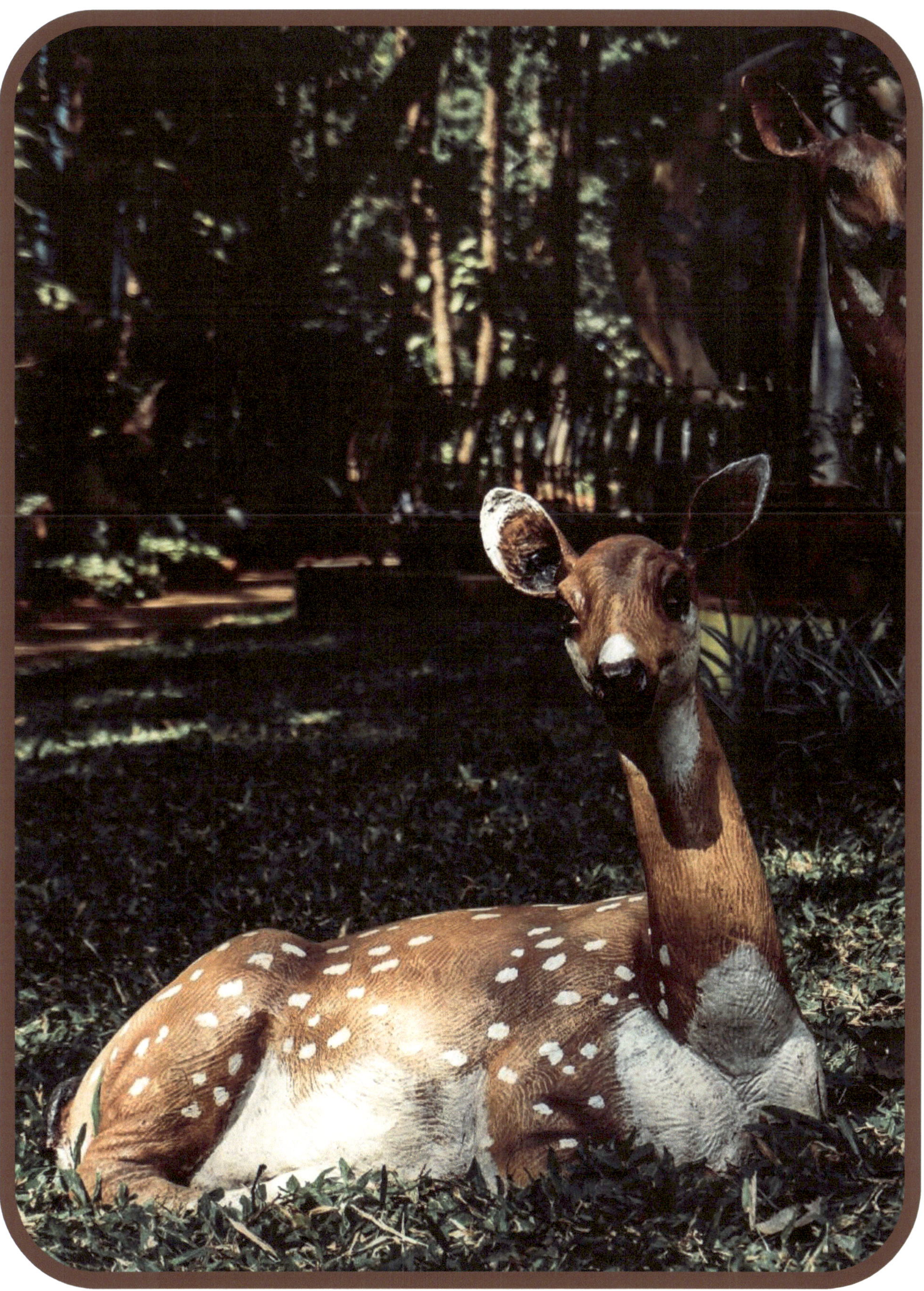

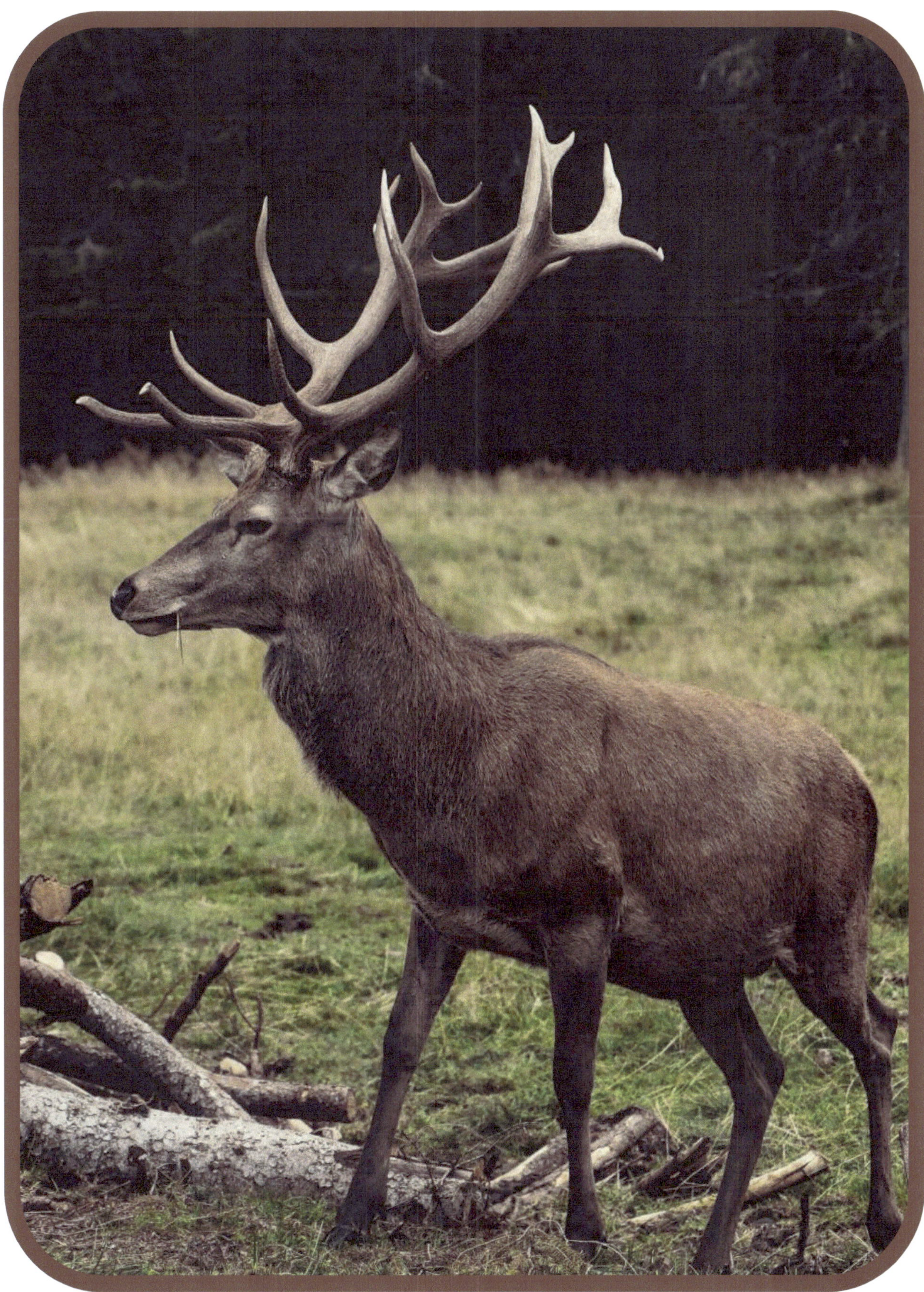

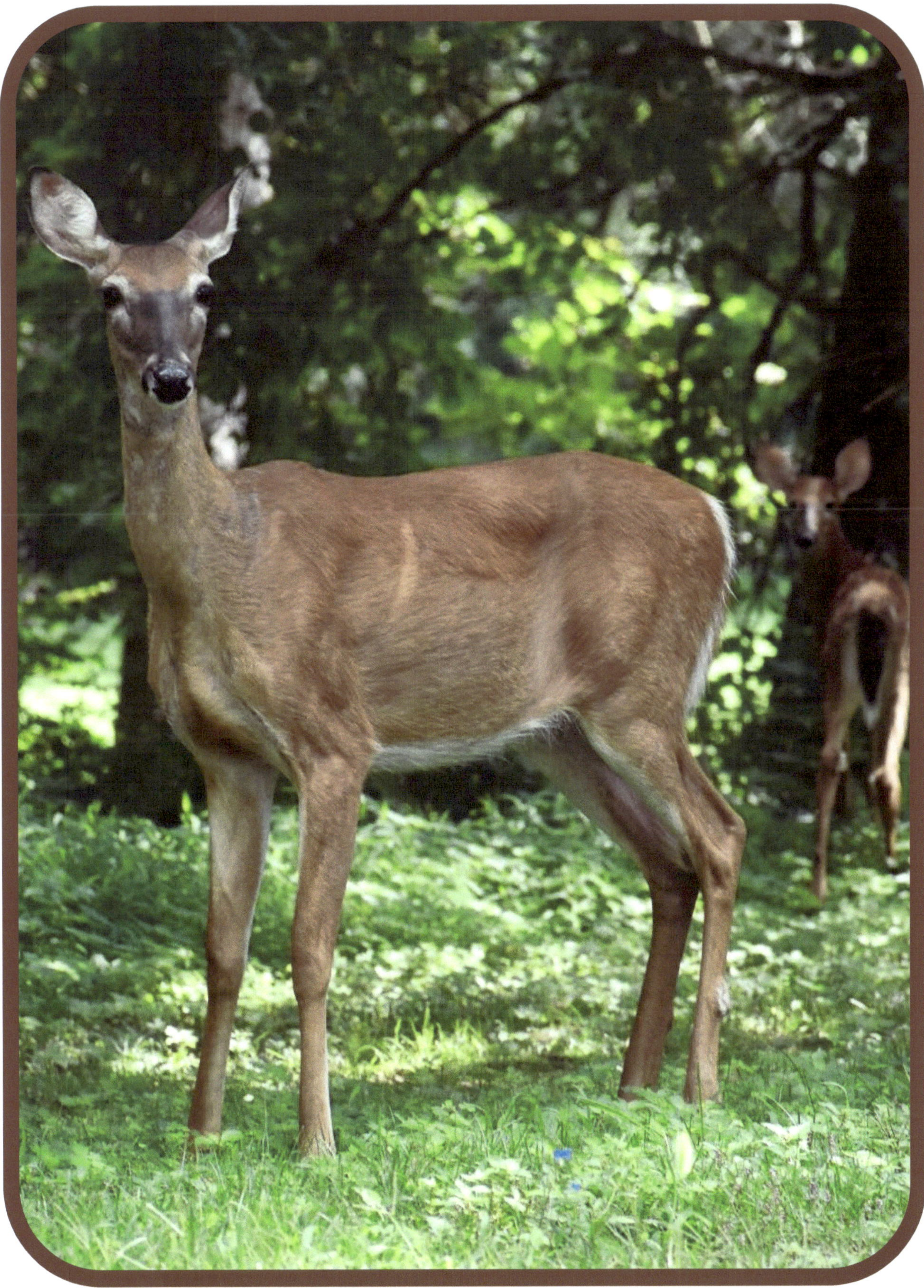

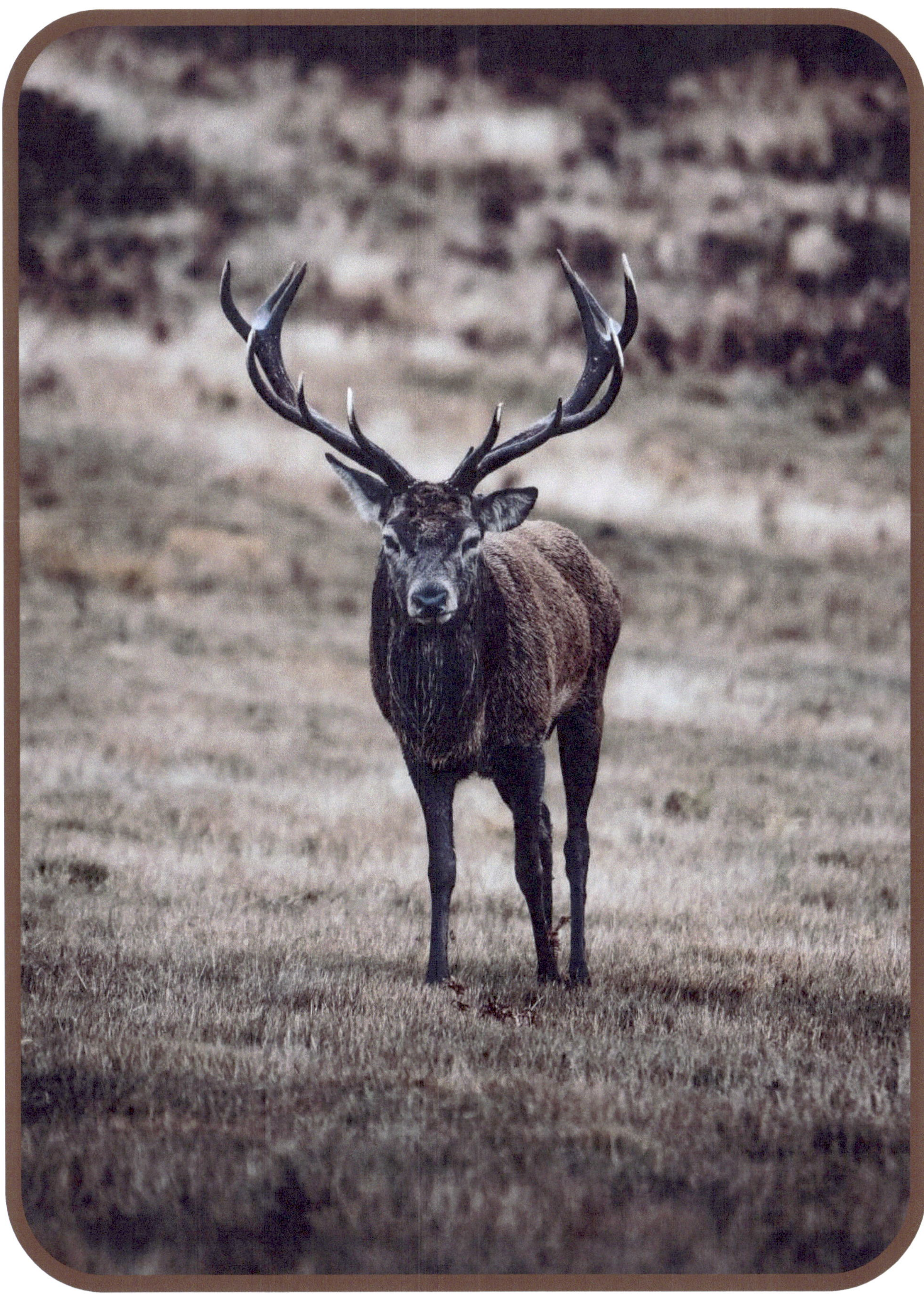

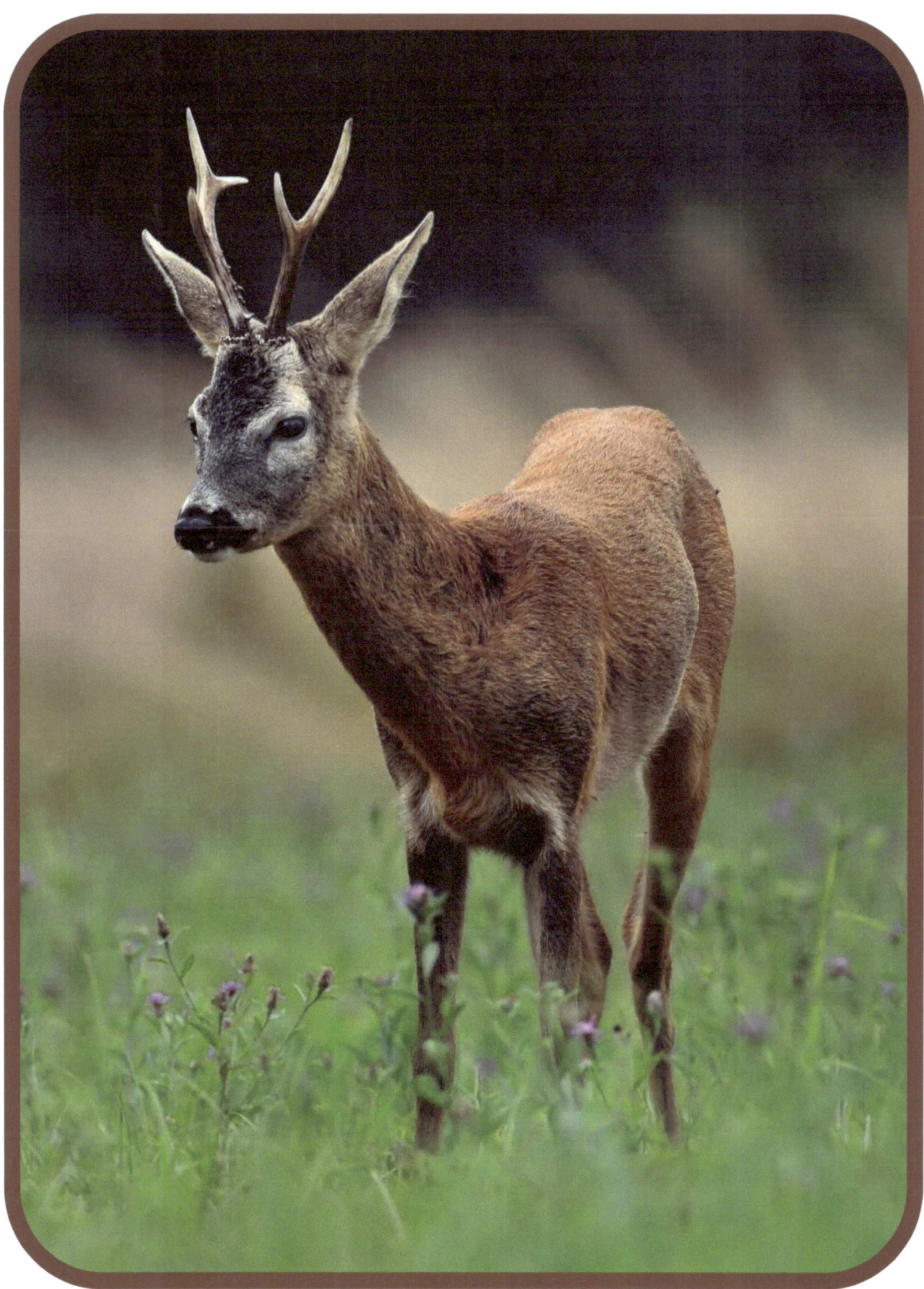

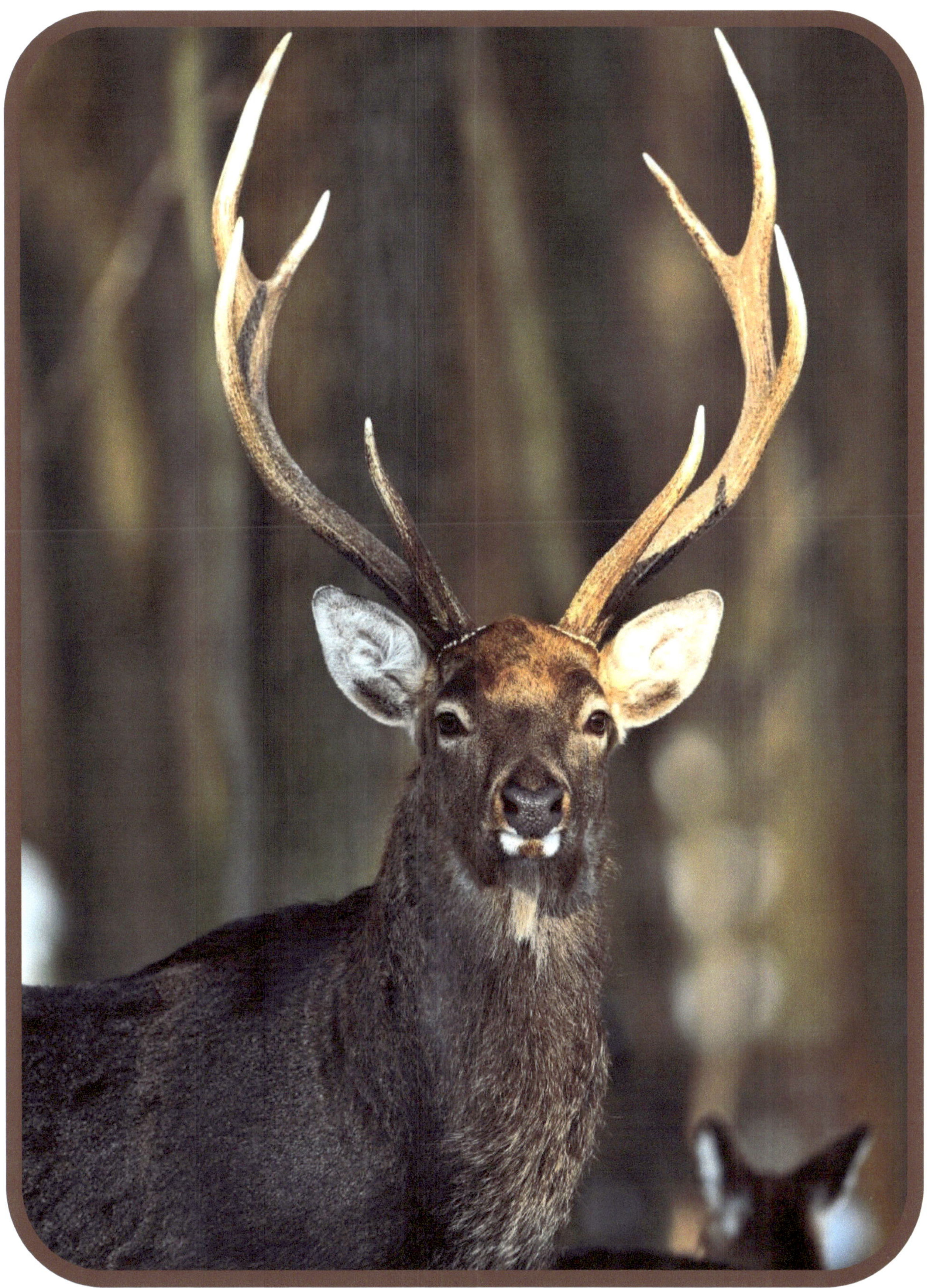

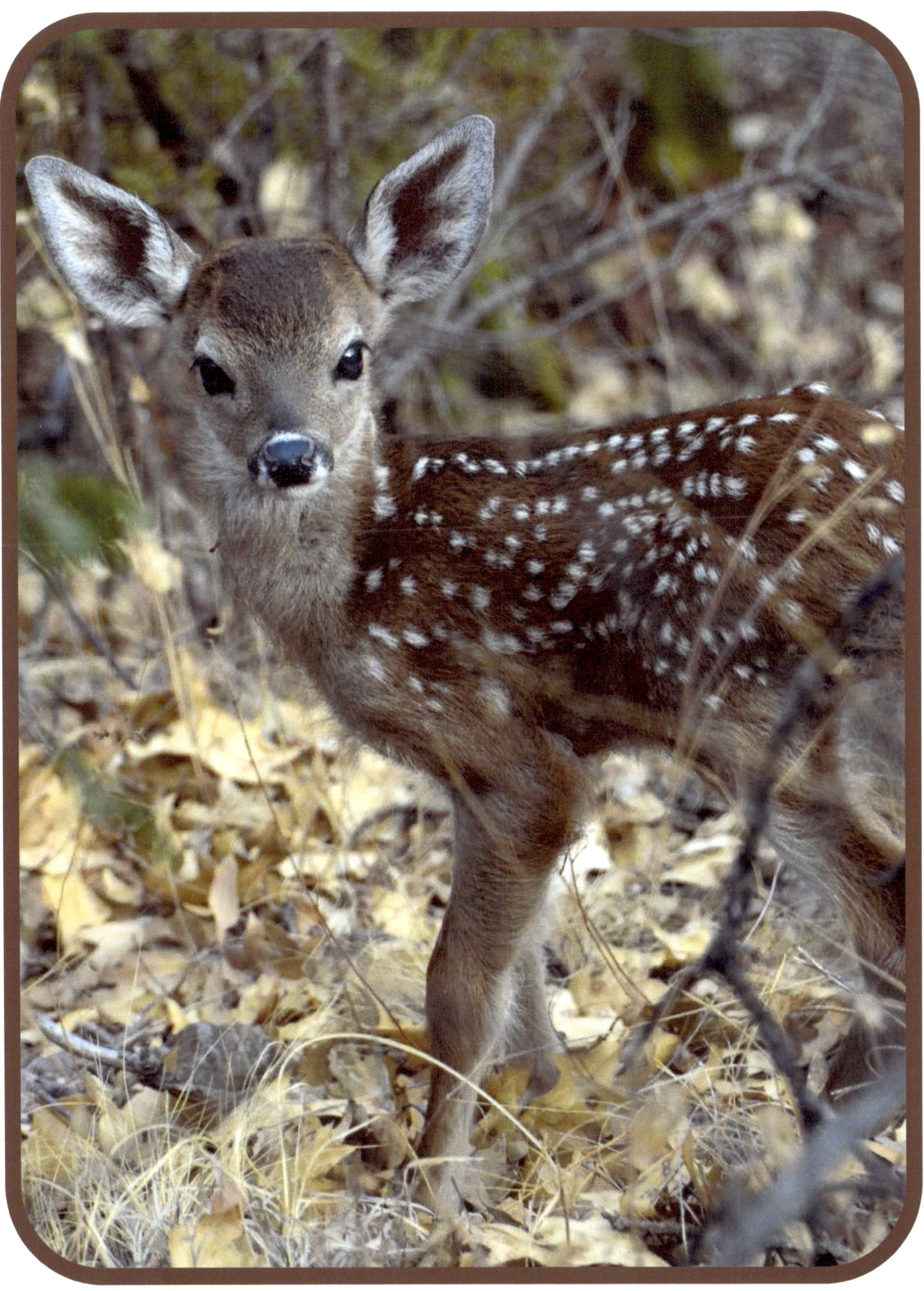

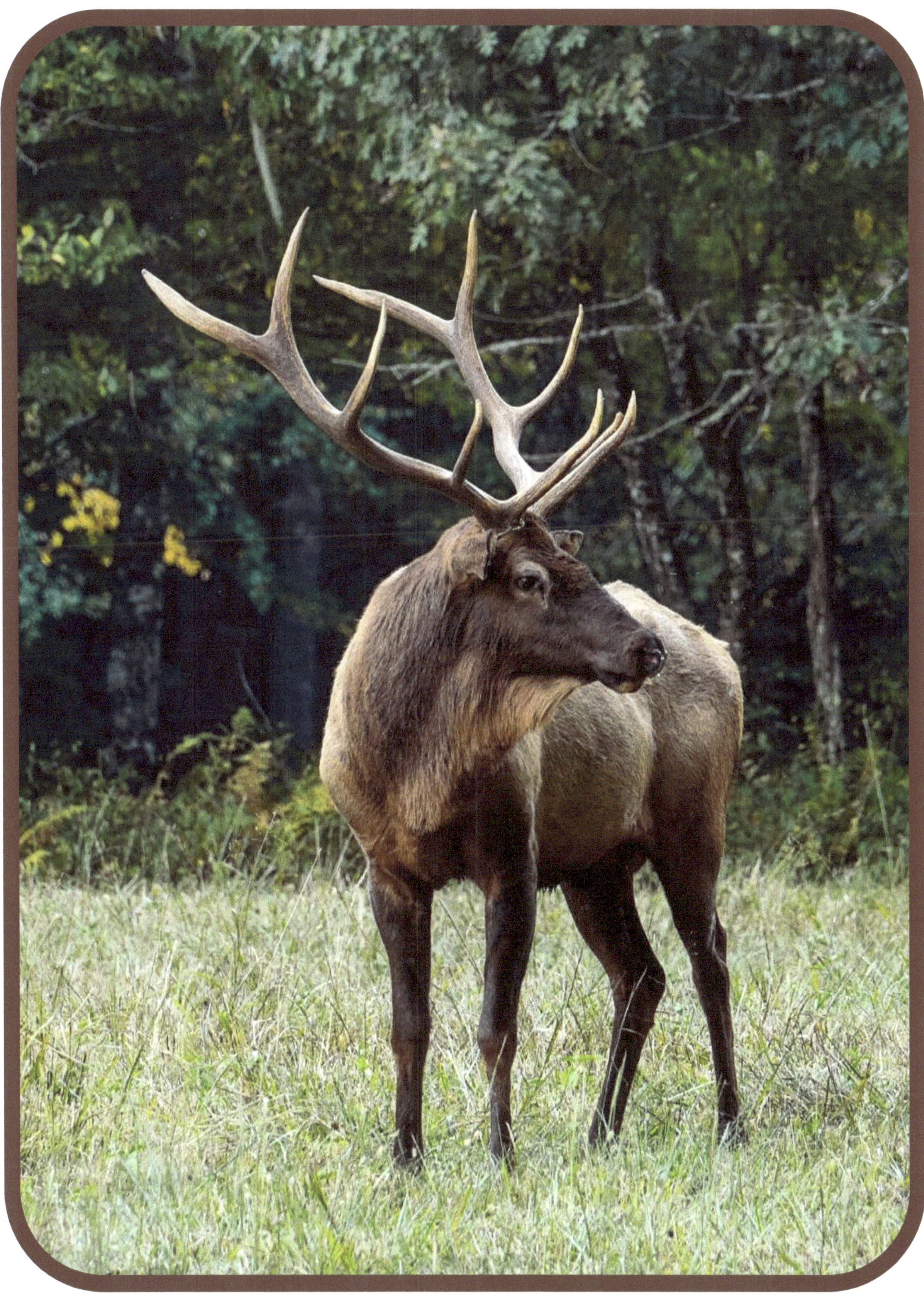

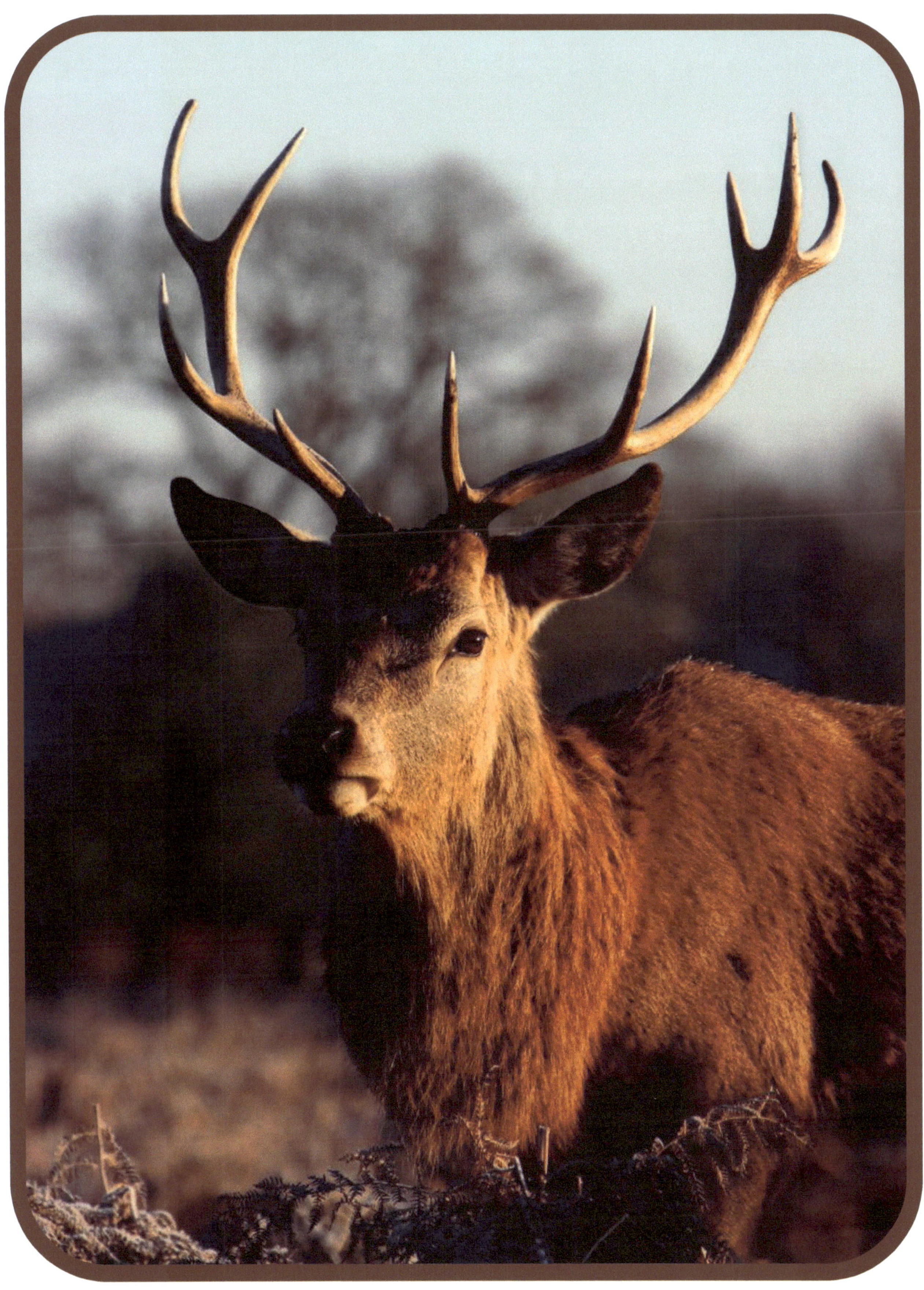

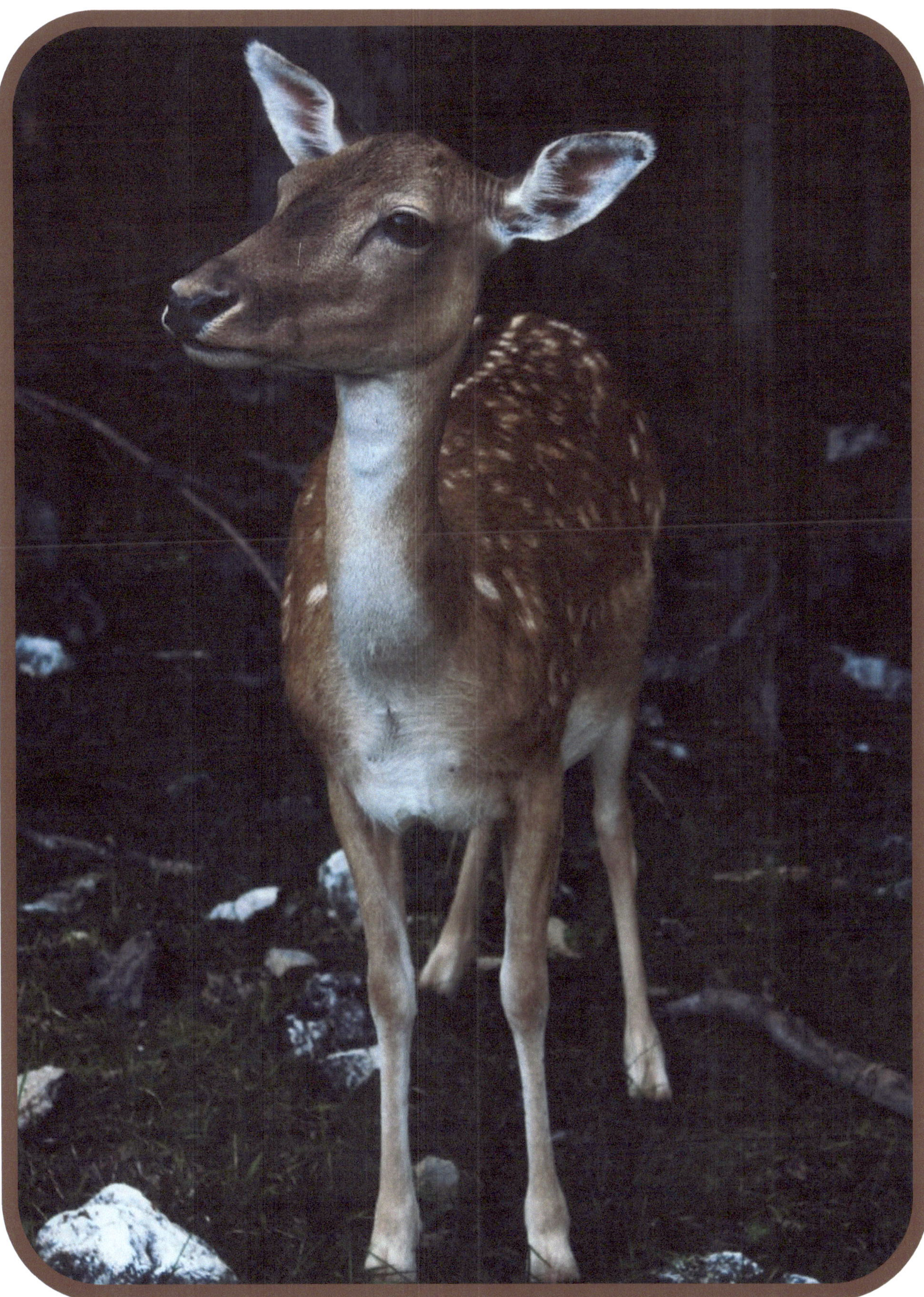

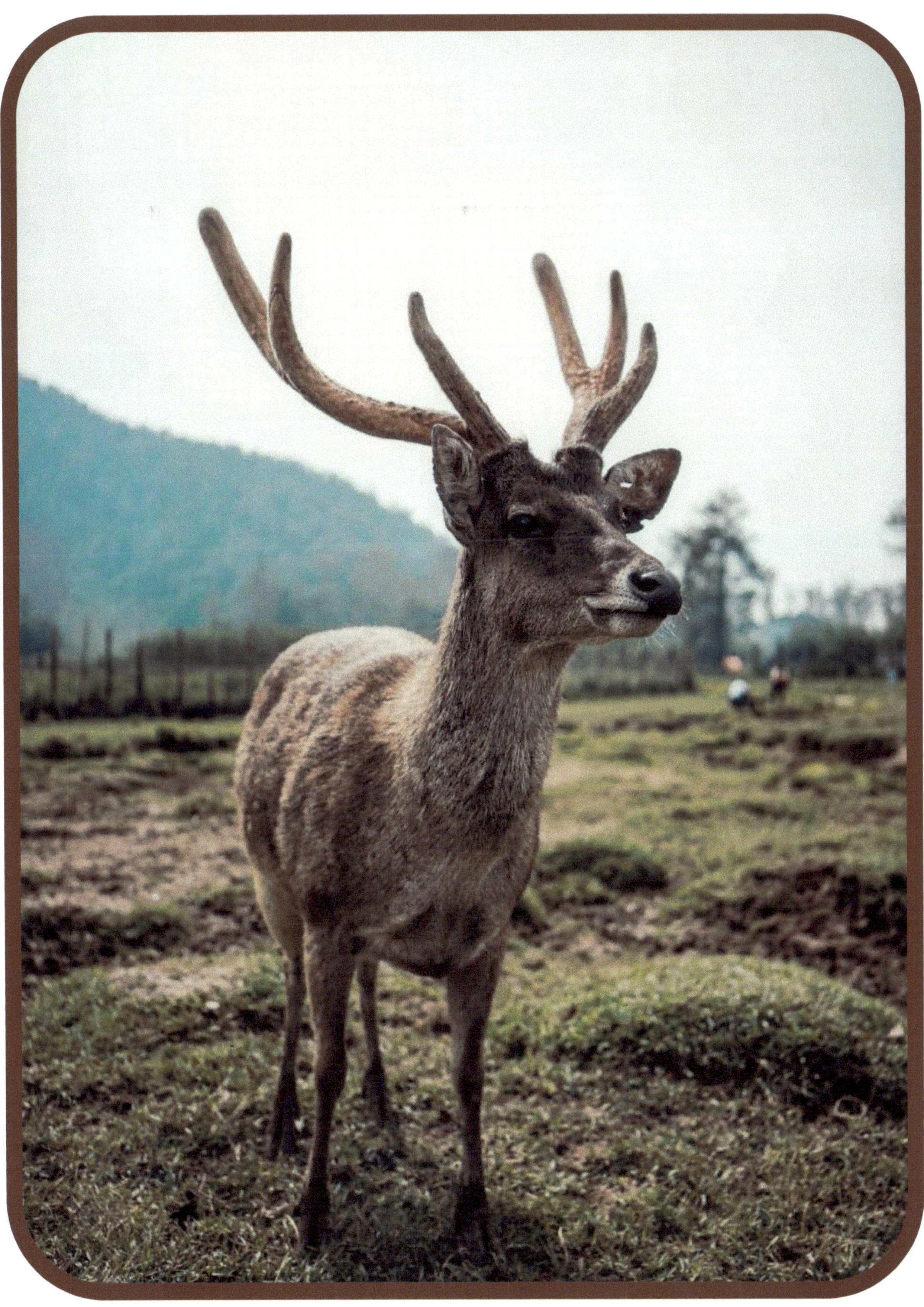

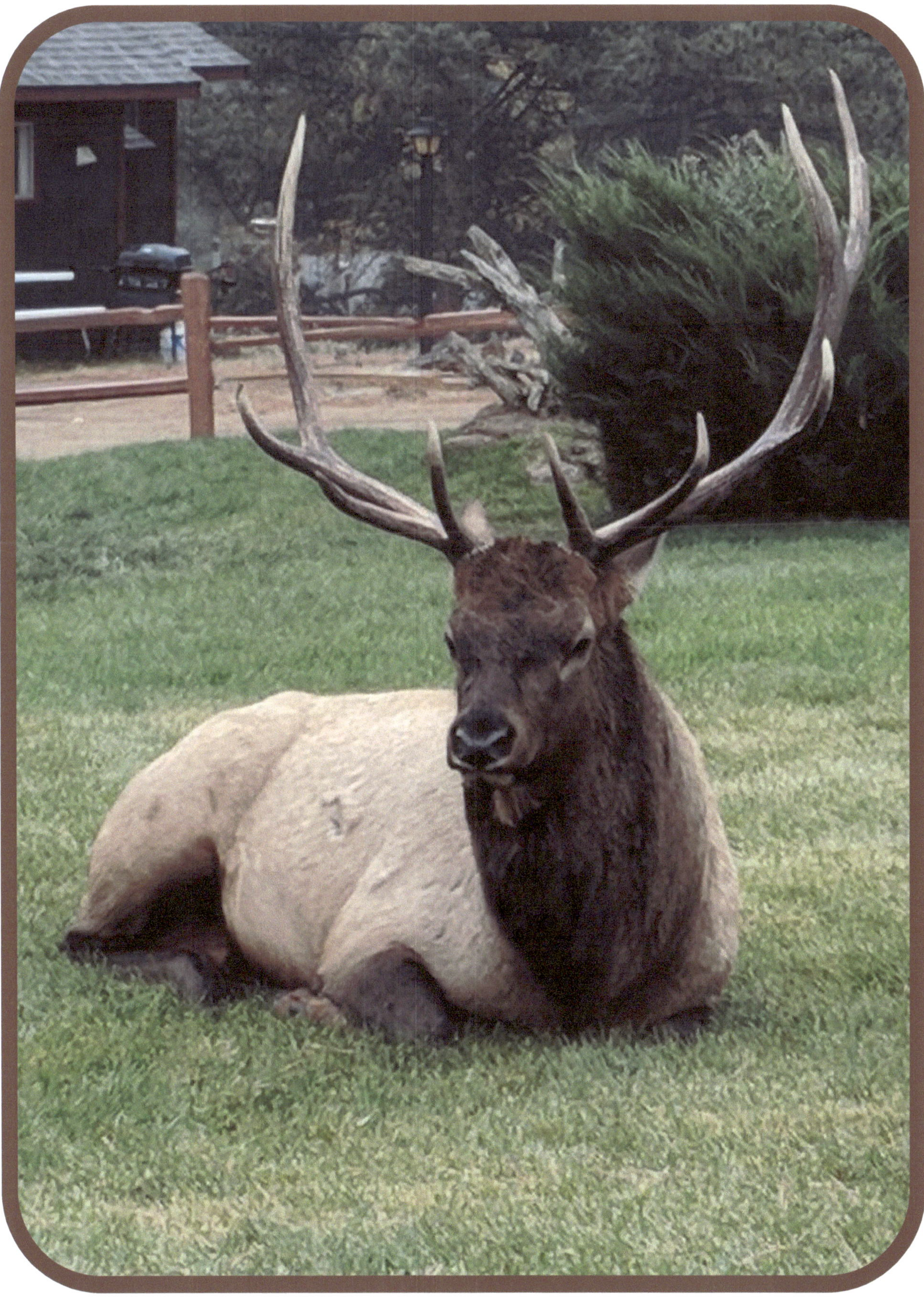